LET THEM GO LIKE A LEADER

Powerful HR Insights for Small Business Owners

DR. ABRAHAM KHOUREIS, PH.D.

Copyright Notice

Table of Contents

Preface

I never set out to write a book about letting people go.

In fact, for most of my life, I have been on the other side, devoted to building people up, mentoring them, guiding them, uplifting them, inspire them, and helping them grow. But in time, I learned something every small business owner eventually faces: leadership is not just about growing people. Sometimes, it is about releasing them, with grace, and compassion, not guilt, and sadness.

Over the years, clients, friends, colleagues, medical, dental, and wellness professionals, shop owners, solo practitioners, have come to me with the same question: "Can you help me let someone go?" Not because they wanted to hurt anyone. But because they cared. Just they did not know how to do it without feeling like a villain.

This book is for them.

I wrote this book for them and for business owners in similar situations.

Let Them Go Like a Leader was written for the quiet leader who loses sleep over hard decisions. For the business owner who wants to protect their team, their business, and their organization, but not at the cost of their reputation and peace. For the person who understands that compassion is not a weakness, it is a form of strength.

Inside, you will find more than steps. You will find real insights for real moments. You are not alone. Because there is a way to lead a business, make the tough calls, and still stay true to your values. That way begins here.

Acknowledgments

Letting someone go with dignity is a leadership act that requires courage, reflection and clarity.

Writing this book was no different. It required courage, reflection, and clarity. And I did not walk this path alone.

Leadership is not a title. It is the quiet decision to do what is right, even when it feels uncomfortable. This book came from over thirty years of that kind of decision-making, earned not in theory, but in real experiences, across seven small businesses I built and led. Every challenge, every reflection, and every conversation with those who came to me for guidance helped shape these pages.

To every small business owner who has ever carried the quiet weight of a hard decision, your strength inspired this book. We are the backbone

3

of economies and the heart of communities. This is for you.

To the professionals who trusted me to walk with them through the highs and lows of your business decisions, your stories live in the spirit of this work. Thank you for letting me witness your leadership in real time.

To the compassionate leaders who believe business can be kind, and who know that letting someone go does not mean letting go of your values, thank you for showing the world a better way.

To my colleagues, students, and clients, thank you for asking honest questions and expecting more from leadership. You pushed me to think deeper, lead better, and teach from the heart.

To the team behind the scenes, my publishing circle, and everyone who believed in this message, your faith gave these words their wings.

To the readers holding this book, I honor your commitment to lead with courage and compassion. You did not come here for empty advice. You came for clarity, direction, and truth. I hope these pages serve you well.

To my family, thank you for your love, patience, and belief in everything I try to build.

With gratitude,

Dr. Abe

This page intentionally left blank for your reading reflection

Introduction

Letting Them Go Is The Most Humane Thing To Do

No one starts a business dreaming about firing someone. We dream of building something meaningful, of offering a service, a product, or a purpose that makes life better for others. We imagine team huddles, success celebrations, maybe even lifelong friendship and mutual brotherly bonds. What we do not imagine, what we never want, is the quiet ache of realizing someone on our team no longer belongs.

Yet, here we are.

If You have picked up this book, you are likely standing at that uncomfortable crossroads: one path feels harsh, the other feels helpless. Do you let your employee, staff or associate go and risk guilt, conflict, or legal entanglements? Or do you keep them, hoping they will change, while your standards, your team, and your peace erode?

This book is here to offer a third path, a clearer one. One that does not abandon kindness and does not confuse it with weakness. One that protects your business, honors your team, and allows you to make hard decisions with courage and compassion.

Because letting go is not always a punishment. Sometimes, it is the most humane thing we can do, for them and for you.

I have seen it up close, dental offices with three employees, wellness centers with five, small family-run shops trying to survive the week. In places like these, every person counts.

Which means when someone does not pull their weight, shows up late, gossips, undermines, or simply does not fit, it shows. Morale drops. Energy shifts. Patients or clients feel it. And still, most leaders hesitate to act.

Why? Because firing someone feels cold. It feels corporate. It feels like giving up.

But what if it did not have to be that way?

What if letting someone go could be a door opened, not slammed shut? What if it could be done with dignity, honesty, and fairness? What if you could protect your company and your conscience?

That is what this book is about. It is not about becoming cold-hearted; it is about becoming clear-hearted. Knowing when to act, how to act, and how to hold space for the humanity of the people involved, including yourself.

Each chapter offers not just policy and paperwork, but also intentional insights with purpose. You will find scripts, checklists, reflections, and real-life wisdom. Not from a distant boardroom, but from real businesses, just like yours.

So, if your heart is heavy with a decision, know this: you are not alone. Leadership is not easy, but it is deeply sacred when done with integrity.

Let us explore it together. One step at a time. With grace, compassion, and strength.

Chapter 1

The Human
In Human Resources

Before the policies, the procedures, the forms, and the checklists, there is a human being. And another. And another. A team made up of lives, not line items.

This is what most small business owners forget when they think about "HR." Or rather, this is what they remember too deeply. Because unlike large corporations, where letting someone go might be someone else's responsibility, here, in your space, in your small business, whether a dental clinic, your studio, your boutique, your wellness center, you *know* your employees. You know who just had a baby, who is fighting anxiety, who is struggling with rent. You have brought them coffee. You have covered for them. You have celebrated their birthdays.

That is what makes "HR" so personal.

So, let us begin by breaking a myth: **Human Resources is not a cold system. I envision it as a practice of responsibility wrapped in compassion.** It is not about being ruthless. It is about being *ready*, to lead, to correct, to support, and, when necessary, to release.

If you have ever felt that strange pit in your stomach when thinking about letting your employee go, that means you care. That is good. But care alone is not enough. Care without clarity becomes chaos. You must know when caring means correcting, and when it means cutting the cord, for the health of the whole.

Let us say this clearly: Letting someone go does not mean you have failed as a leader. It often means you are finally stepping into your leadership fully.

The Cost of Avoidance

In my years working with leaders in small practices and corporate ones alike, I have seen what happens when owners and leaders avoid the hard conversation. They delay. They hope. They tolerate. In the process, they:

- Lose the trust of their loyal employees.

- Damage their business reputation with clients.

- Experience burnout trying to "make up" for the employee's gaps.

The truth is, one weak link can weaken the chain. Especially in small teams. You do not need a dozen problematic employees to derail your business. You **only need one**, and your silence will be interpreted as approval.

Why You are Here

You are reading this book because you want to do things right. You want to protect your business and your soul. You do not want to hurt anyone. But you are also done being hurt by indecision. That is not just noble, it is wise.

This book would not teach you how to become an HR, business or legal expert overnight, nor will it pretend you need to be a hardened executive. I wrote it with the purpose of sharing with you how to lead with a backbone and a heart.

We will walk through every step:

- How to document concerns.
- How to confront performance issues.
- How to prepare for a possible termination.

- And how to handle that conversation with courage and care.

You will also learn how to build systems that prevent future confusion: clear contracts, early expectations, soft corrections, and stronger hiring practices.

Let us put Human in Human Resources

Before we go further, promise yourself this: **You would not become robotic in the name of policy.** You will protect your business, but you will also protect your values. You will speak kindly. You will act fairly. You will sleep well. Because the most compassionate thing you can sometimes do, for everyone, is let someone go.

You are here to protect the organizational ecosystem you have built. A business with a culture. A team with trust. A place where people come to work, grow, serve, and find pride in what they do.

Let us build that together. It begins here, with you, the human at the heart of it all.

Chapter 2

Small Business
Big Responsibility

In large corporations, HR is a department. In small businesses, HR is you.

You do not have a legal team downstairs. You do not have an HR manager to handle hard conversations. There is no employee relations officer or compliance specialist waiting in the wings.

There is just you, and maybe a partner, a receptionist, a bookkeeper, and the courage to build something meaningful with very little margin for error.

This is the truth many small business owners face:

You wear every hat. Some of them do not fit because you are not fit and trained enough to wear them.

You did not go into dentistry or retail or wellness to become an expert in labor law or workplace investigations. You built your business to serve. But along the way, you became the person others now look to for answers. Fairness. Boundaries. Protection.

That is no small responsibility.
You Are the System.

In your business, there is no buffer between you and your team. You are the policy. You are the structure. You are the support. If you are not intentional, you will be reactive.

That is why you need to lead like a department of one, with just enough structure to function, just enough clarity to protect yourself and your people, and just enough wisdom to know when to ask for help.

You do not need to memorize state statutes. But you do need to know the basics:

- How and when to document employee concerns.

- What is required when you terminate someone.

- What benefits, breaks, and protections your state mandates.

- How to protect yourself from claims of discrimination or retaliation.

- How to write a job description that covers more than just tasks.

You can outsource legal advice. You can hire consultants. But day to day, you are the one who sets the tone and holds the line.

What You Can Do Today

You do not need a full HR department, but you do need a few solid tools:

1. An employee file for each person: include their application, job description, signed offer letter, handbook acknowledgment, and any written warnings.

2. A simple handbook: cover attendance, communication, conflict resolution, time off, and expectations of conduct.

3. A written process for hiring and termination, even if it is just one page.

4. Outside help on call: an attorney, HR consultant, or payroll provider who can advise when things get complicated.

Most of all, have a **mirror policy**: do not expect from your employees what you would not model yourself.

You will not always get it right. You will make messy decisions, miss red flags, wait too long to act, or act too soon out of frustration. That is human. What matters is how quickly you learn and how honestly you course-correct.

HR is not about perfection. It is about protecting people, including you.

Running a business is already a risk. Leading people adds another layer. Do not shrink from it. Rise into it. Read what you need to read. Ask questions when you are unsure. Let mistakes humble you, not harden you.

Because every time you handle a tough conversation with fairness, you are not just growing your business, you are growing yourself.

In a small business, your leadership shows up in the quiet moments. In how you address lateness. In how you handle gossip. In how you praise, how you correct, and how you let people go.

You do not need a degree in HR. You just need courage, clarity, and compassion.

Chapter 3

Building a Compassionate Company

Letting someone go with grace is important. But building a compassionate culture where people rarely have to be let go, that is the real legacy.

Culture is not a banner on a wall. It is not the words you say during team meetings. It is what your people feel when they walk in the door. It is how safe they feel to speak up. How willing they are to admit mistakes. How clear they are on what matters.

A compassionate culture does not mean everyone agrees. It means everyone matters. It does not mean there is no accountability. It means there is fairness, respect, and understanding behind every decision.

You do not need a large company to build that kind of culture. In fact, **small businesses are uniquely positioned to do it best**, because everything is close, personal, and real.

Where Culture Lives

Culture shows up in the in-between:

- How you greet people in the morning.

- How you respond when someone's struggling

- How conflict is handled.

- Whether praise is public and correction is private.

- Whether leadership models the behavior it asks for.

It is not what you post on your website. It is what you practice when no one is watching.

Three Pillars of a Compassionate Culture

1. Clarity

Without clear expectations, even good people feel lost.

> Be consistent in your standards.
>
> Define roles. Communicate changes.
>
> Address issues early.
>
> Clarity removes guessing and guessing leads to fear.

2. Connection

Your team needs to feel seen. Know their names, not just their titles. Celebrate small wins. Say thank you. Make space for their stories.

Connection builds loyalty, and loyal teams protect the culture with you.

3. Care

Do not wait for someone to fall apart to show kindness. Show it in structure. Show it in second chances. Show it in how you lead hard conversations without shame.

Care does not mean being soft. It means being steady, honest and humane at once.

The Culture You Tolerate Is the One You Build

Every behavior you ignore becomes part of your culture. Every off comment, every broken rule, every eye-roll that goes unchecked, it all adds up.

But every act of alignment, every boundary held with kindness, every difficult decision made with integrity, builds a culture people want to stay in.

You are always building culture. The question is:

Are you building it by design or by default?

When You Get It Wrong, Repair

No leader gets it right every time. You will say the wrong thing. You will avoid a conversation too long. You will trust the wrong person. That does not destroy culture, unless you ignore it.

Own your mistakes. Apologize when needed. Repair when possible. Your team does not need a perfect boss. They need an honest one.

The Long-Term View

A compassionate culture does not just reduce turnover. It attracts the right people. It encourages innovation. It creates a space where people give their best because they feel safe, not scared.

And you? You get to lead without becoming someone you are not. You get to be both decisive and kind. Strong and understanding. You get to sleep at night knowing you built something that reflects your values, not just your goals.

That is the kind of business that endures.

You have now walked the full path, from hiring wisely, to setting expectations, to letting go with grace like a leader, and now, to building something that lasts.

Letting go may be the hardest thing a leader does. But building a compassionate company culture? That is the most powerful.

Chapter 4

Hiring with Eyes Open

Most hiring mistakes happen before a single question is asked.

They happen when we are rushed, desperate, or distracted. When a team member quits without notice. When a business grows faster than expected. When we hire out of pressure, not purpose.

But in a small business, every hire is a heartbeat. The wrong one disrupts the entire rhythm. And unlike a corporate giant, you do not have the luxury of absorbing poor performance into the background. In your space, it shows. It shakes trust. It affects client experience. It affects *you*.

So, how do we stop hiring with our eyes half-closed?

We slow down. We get honest. And we remember this: **You are not just filling a role; you are inviting someone into a very delicate ecosystem.**

Look Beyond the Resume:

A pristine resume means very little if the person behind it lacks character, accountability, or emotional intelligence. Especially in intimate team settings, your new hire needs to be more than qualified, they need to be *compatible*.

Before you hire them, ask yourself:

- Will this person bring harmony or drama?

- Do they show signs of self-awareness?

- Are they teachable?

- Will clients trust them instinctively?

You can teach technical skills. You cannot teach values.

So, stop hiring only for skill, hire for **fit, integrity, and vibe**. The people you hire will shape your business atmosphere more than your logo ever will.

Red Flags in Disguise:

You know them. The sweet-talker who name-drops but never listens. The overly eager candidate who avoids answering directly. The one who only speaks about what they want but never asks what the team needs.

These are not just annoying quirks, they are warning signs.

In small businesses, manipulation, entitlement, and gossip do not stay tucked away in a corner, they grow like mold. So, trust your gut. If you feel an off energy in the interview, *do not ignore it* just because their experience looks good on paper.

If you feel torn and feel that you must make a decision, delay the hire. You will lose less money from a delayed start than from months of damage control.

Ask Better Questions:

Move beyond "Tell me about yourself." Ask:

- "What do you think makes a team healthy?"

- "How do you handle being corrected?"

- "What is something your last manager would say you need to work on?"

Their answers won't just tell you about them, they will show you how honest and emotionally mature they are.

Define What You are Really Hiring For:

Is it just a receptionist, or the face of your office or clinic?
Is it just an assistant, or the emotional thermostat of your team?

Is it just a hygienist, or someone who will reassure nervous patients?

Define the deeper function, then hire someone who can *live* that, not just perform tasks.

Include Your Team:

If your current team is healthy, involve them. Have a second or third person meet the candidate. Ask what they sensed. Sometimes, your staff sees what you overlook.

But only do this if your team is mature. Otherwise, you risk bias creeping into your decision.

No Hire Is Better Than a Bad Hire:

Say this to yourself until it is memorized: **You are not behind, you are being deliberate.**

Hiring someone who does not align will cost you far more in morale, energy, and time than leaving the role open for a little longer.

So, hire with eyes wide open. Choose with your mind and your heart aligned. Remember, you are not just building a business. You are building a sanctuary for good people to do meaningful work.

One person at a time.

Chapter 5

The Foundation, Clear Expectations

Before any employee fails, expectations fail first.

Miscommunication does not usually begin with words; it begins with assumptions. As a business owner, especially in small teams, it is easy to assume others "just know" how things are supposed to be. But they do not. Not really. They interpret. They guess. They operate based on past environments, personal comfort, or best intentions. And when that does not align with your expectations, friction begins.

But clarity? Clarity is kindness.

It is what allows people to succeed or step aside. It reduces confusion, prevents conflict, and gives you a clear standard to return to when something goes wrong.

Without it, you are not leading, you are hoping.

Clarity Is a Leader's First Language

Whether your business has three employees or thirty, your expectations should be as clear as your branding, as consistent as your hours, and as visible as your storefront.

Start here:

- What does "on time" mean? Five minutes early? Walking in at the exact minute?

- What does "good communication" look like? Weekly updates? Proactive check-ins?

- What are your non-negotiables? Phone use? Uniform? Attitude toward clients?

If you cannot define it, do not expect it.

The Job Description Is Your First Shield

A solid job description is not just a hiring tool, it is a protection tool. It sets the parameters, roles, and boundaries from day one. It gives both you and the employee something to return to when there is doubt or disagreement.

Include:

- Core responsibilities.

- Expected behavior (such as tone, presence, communication style).

- Daily, weekly, and monthly tasks.

- Who they report to.

- Measures of success.

- Terms of evaluation.

This does not make your workplace rigid. It

makes it safe. When people know what is expected, they can rise to meet it, or respectfully admit they are not the right fit.

The First Week Sets the Tone

Do not wait for a problem to train someone. Train on day one. Walk them through:

- How to open and close the office.

- How you want them to communicate with clients.

- What they do during downtime.

- What happens if they are running late or feeling sick.

- How feedback is given and received.

It is not about micromanaging. It is about setting a rhythm early, one that protects them and you. Do not assume they know, because probably they do not.

Put It in Writing. Every Time.

Verbal instructions fade. Written guidelines remain.

Keep a simple, readable employee handbook. No jargon. Just clear policies, responsibilities, and rights. Add a signature page to confirm they have read and understood it.

This is not about formality, it is about memory. When things feel shaky later, you will both have something to return to.

Expectations Are Not Just About Performance

Too often, leaders only focus on the task. But behavior matters just as much.

Set expectations for:

- How we treat one another.

- How we handle client complaints.

- How we bring up concerns or disagreements.

- What accountability looks like on this team.

This builds a culture, not just a company. When that culture is consistent, it becomes self-sustaining.

Update as You Grow

Your expectations will evolve as your business grows. Do not let outdated systems linger. Review your handbook once a year. Adjust roles as you delegate more. Update job descriptions when technology or workflow changes.

Stagnant expectations lead to resentment. Evolving ones show leadership.

Compassion Does not Cancel Clarity

Sometimes we think being kind means being soft. But real kindness includes telling the truth, early and respectfully.

Let your team know:

- You will always be clear.

- You will always be fair.

- And you expect the same in return.

This builds mutual respect. It lets people succeed by design, not luck.

Chapter 6

How to Train Your HR Mindset

Human resources is not a department. It is a mindset. It is the daily practice of how people are hired, guided, inspired, challenged, and, when needed, let go. For many small business owners, HR is something to deal with only when things go wrong. But what if it became a leadership strength instead of a management burden?

To lead with an HR mindset is to see people as your greatest asset. It means building habits, systems, and culture around growth, fairness, clarity, and compassion. This chapter offers a practical guide to developing that mindset, whether you have a team of two or twenty.

From Reactive to Proactive

Many owners only focus on HR when they must fire someone, address drama, or respond to a claim. That is reactive HR. A proactive mindset, by contrast, builds a strong people foundation from day one.

Here is what it means to shift into proactive HR:

- Hire with clarity, not just speed.

- Create onboarding experiences, not just orientations.

- Give feedback early and regularly, not just during crises.

- Put values and expectations in writing.

- Recognize great work out loud.

- Notice burnout before it explodes.

This shift changes everything, from morale to retention to productivity.

Developing HR Awareness

1. An HR mindset does not require an HR title. It requires attention to five key areas:

2. Hiring Practices

   Are you hiring with a clear role, fair process, and honest communication? Or are you winging it and hoping for the best?

3. Performance Culture

Do your team members know what success looks like? Do they receive guidance, recognition, and course correction?

4. Policies and Boundaries

   Have you established fair and written policies? Are expectations known and consistently applied?

5. Conflict Response

Are you willing to step in early and calmly? Do you address friction with curiosity rather than avoidance?

6. Compassionate Exits

Do you have a graceful plan for when someone must leave, one that protects their dignity and your integrity?

How to Build Your HR Muscles

- Block time for people, not just problems.

- Create a simple HR checklist and revisit it monthly.

- Talk to other business owners about what they have learned.

- Take one online HR course, just one.

- Assign one person (even part-time) to help carry the HR load.

You do not need to do everything at once. You just need to care enough to begin.

Why It Matters

People decisions are business decisions. Who you hire, how you coach, when you let go, these choices shape your culture, reputation, and results. An HR mindset is not soft. It is strategic.

When owners develop their HR instincts, their teams thrive. Turnover drops. Trust grows. And the business runs with greater ease, because people feel seen, safe, and respected.

Lead like a small business owner, yes. But also lead like a head of people. Because in truth, that is what you are.

> Train your mindset. Lead with heart. Grow your people as fiercely as you grow your profits. That is what it means to let them go, like a leader.

Chapter 7

When HR Is You

In many small businesses, there is no formal HR department. There is no head of people, no compliance officer, and no dedicated specialist managing the employee journey. There is only you, the owner, the operator, the leader. And in these cases, HR is not a role you delegate. It is one you live.

When HR is you, the rules shift. There is no one else to blame for a poor hire or an unfair dismissal. There is no buffer between your emotions and your decisions. There is only your intent, your action, and the ripple effect they create.

This chapter is for those who wear every hat. The founder who signs the paychecks and also writes the job descriptions. The manager who fields customer complaints and also listens to employee frustrations. The business owner who hopes to build a great team but feels unsure how to handle HR with fairness, legality, and compassion.

The Myth of Wearing All Hats

Yes, you wear many hats. But when it comes to HR, you cannot afford to treat it as just another one. Human Resources, when done well, is not just a task, it is a function of leadership. It is how you communicate expectations, build culture, and create safety.

You may not have an HR title, but you have HR power. Every decision you make, who to hire, how to evaluate, when to promote, and if someone must go, builds or breaks trust.

The myth is that HR is external. The truth is: HR is leadership in action.

When You Are the Policy

In small businesses, people do not open a handbook, they look at you. They read your tone. They watch your consistency. They listen to how you speak about others when they are not in the room. They observe whether you practice what you preach.

If you want a fair workplace, you must model fairness. If you want transparency, be transparent. If you value growth, offer it. The policies you may not have written yet are already being lived through your behavior.

So ask yourself: what kind of HR are you showing?

Balancing Heart and Accountability

Leading with heart does not mean avoiding accountability. It means delivering it with dignity. When HR is you, you have to create the balance:

- Be kind, but do not ignore red flags.

- Be flexible, but do not be inconsistent.

- Be supportive, but do not tolerate harm to others.

A compassionate HR leader does not shy away from consequences. Instead, they apply them with clarity and fairness.

Know the Basics, Stay Out of Trouble

Even if you are a people-first leader, there are HR basics you must know to stay compliant and protect your business. These include:

- Understanding at-will employment laws.

- Documenting job expectations and feedback.

- Keeping personnel files secure and organized.

- Offering appropriate accommodations when needed.

- Handling payroll, taxes, and benefits properly.

- Ensuring no discrimination, retaliation, or favoritism occurs.

Ignorance is not innocence in the eyes of the law. You do not need to become an expert, but you do need to learn. Resources, advisors, and workshops exist to support you, use them.

Build Mini Systems

You do not need a massive HR operation to run a healthy workplace. What you need are mini systems:

- A checklist for onboarding new hires.

- A process for handling time-off requests.

- A template for giving performance feedback.

- A calendar reminder for annual evaluations.

Systems give your employees clarity. They give you peace of mind. They reduce emotional guesswork and increase professionalism.

Document, Always

Whether it is a conversation, an agreement, or a warning, document it. Not to build a case, but to build clarity. Write things down when they happen, and store them in a private, secure place. If you ever need to make a hard decision, you will have a story of what led there.

The Leader as Culture Keeper

Culture is not a poster on the wall. It is the behavior you tolerate and the values you live. When HR is you, you are not just managing tasks, you are curating an experience. That experience tells your team whether they matter, whether they are safe, and whether they want to stay.

So lead like HR is watching, because it is. Through your people's eyes.

Final Thought

When HR is you, the responsibility is enormous, but so is the opportunity. You get to build a workplace where people feel seen, respected, and empowered. You get to lead with both courage and care.

And one day, when your business grows, and you hire someone to officially run HR, you will already know how to lead them well, because you were HR all along.

Chapter 8

Warning Signs and Gentle Confrontations

A storm rarely comes without a shift in the wind. The same is true in your workplace.

Before someone's behavior becomes a crisis, it sends signals. A shift in tone. A slip in commitment. A growing tension others start to feel but cannot quite name. Most leaders notice it, then wait. They hope it passes. They give benefit after benefit of the doubt. They carry the weight of silence far too long.

But silence is not compassion. It is avoidance wearing a kind face.

In a small team, one person's slow unraveling becomes everyone's burden. That is why you must learn to notice early and respond early, gently, but directly. Because what you allow is what you endorse.

The Small Things Are the Big Things

Warning signs often show up in small ways:

- Chronic lateness that grows from occasional to habitual.

- A change in energy, withdrawn, passive, snappy, or sarcastic.

- Subtle eye-rolls in meetings, or sighs when asked to help.

- Missed details or unfinished tasks.

- Talking over others or undermining coworkers subtly, microaggressions.

- Gossip, cliques, or coldness in the break room.

Each may seem minor in isolation. But when you feel them, something is shifting beneath. Do not wait for it **to explode. Step in while the volume is still low.**

Your Role Is not to Punish, it is to Protect

You are not confronting someone to win. You are addressing something to protect your team, your business, and the dignity of everyone involved.

That mindset shifts your tone. It calms your nerves. It reminds you: this is not personal, it is professional. If done right, it can even be healing.

Begin with Curiosity, Not Accusation

Start softly, but honestly.

Try:

- "I have noticed some changes lately. Can we talk about how things are going?"

- "There's a shift in how tasks are being handled. Is something on your mind?"

- "I have seen you come in late a few times, and I want to make sure everything's okay."

This opens a door instead of slamming one. You are showing concern, not coming down like a hammer.

If they respond well, guide them toward accountability. If they deflect, deny, or react defensively, keep the boundary firm.

Do not Get Trapped in Their Story

Empathy is essential. But it must have a boundary.

If an employee is always "just going through something," and that something never seems to pass, be kind, but be clear. Life happens. But work still needs to function. A team member's personal situation cannot become an excuse for perpetual underperformance.

Say it like this:

- "I hear you, and I care. But we still need to find a way forward that works for the team."

- "Let us talk about how to get back on track. I want to support you, but I also need to see change."

You are showing heart and holding the line. That is leadership. That is what I call showing compassion with strength.

Document Gently but Consistently

Write it down. Even informal conversations should have a short summary: date, issue, tone, and next steps.

You are not creating a file to use against them. You are keeping track in case patterns continue, and in case tough decisions must be made later. Documentation protects everyone's memory from confusion or denial.

Set a Check-In Date

Accountability without a time frame is just a wish.

End the conversation with clear next steps:

- "Let us reconnect in one week to see how things are improving."

- "I'll follow up in a few days. Let us both stay open and honest."

Short timelines create movement. Long ones create forgetfulness.

Do not Let Fear Block Your Leadership

Many business owners wait too long to confront behavior. They are afraid of being unfair, afraid of hurting feelings, afraid of being sued. But the longer you wait, the harder the conversation becomes. And the more damage is done.

You are not being harsh. You are being clear. You are not acting from anger. You are acting from care. If that person truly is not meant to stay, your early honesty will help them find that direction sooner, for their sake and yours.

Say what needs to be said. Say it gently. Say it early. Say it with your shoulders back and your heart open.

That is what a good leader does.

Chapter 9

A Toxic Employee Harm Your Business and The Entire Organization

You could have the best business plan. The most loyal clients. The most beautiful office and the most brilliant vision. But one toxic employee, just one, can undo all of it.

In small businesses, toxicity is not diluted. It is concentrated. It spreads fast. It colors the atmosphere, infects the culture, and quietly turns trust into tension. And the worst part? It does not always look dramatic.

Toxicity does not always scream. Sometimes it whispers. Sometimes it rolls its eyes. Sometimes it plays the victim. Sometimes it simply does not care.

If you do not address it, it does not just stay. It *multiplies*.

What Toxic Looks Like, Beyond the Obvious

Toxicity is not always the loud, hostile employee. Sometimes It is the charming one who manipulates. The quiet one who isolates others. The talented one who disrespects everyone because they "know their value." It may look like:

- Constant complaints with no solutions.

- Undermining authority, policies, or peers.

- Gossiping that divides teams.

- Passive resistance, smiling, then sabotaging.

- Playing favorites or cliques that exclude.

- Taking credit, avoiding responsibility.

If you find yourself saying, "They're good at what they do, but…", stop. The "but" is the sign. Good work does not excuse bad behavior.

The Ripple Effect Is Real

Toxicity affects:

- Morale. Good employees start to dread work.

- Productivity. Time is lost managing emotional fallout.

- Retention. Your best people quietly leave to escape the negativity.

- Clients. They can feel the tension. They will take their business somewhere that feels better.

It affects *you*. You start questioning yourself. You feel drained. You lose joy in your own business. You tiptoe in your own workplace.

That is no way to lead.

Why It is Hard to Let Them Go

Toxic employees often survive longer than they should because:

- They are high performers in some areas.

- They've been with you a long time.

- You feel guilty or obligated.

- You are afraid of confrontation or conflict.

- You hope they will magically change.

But hoping is not a plan. The longer you wait, the more damage they do, and the more complicit you become in their behavior.

The Hard Truth: You Must Choose the Group Over the One

In small teams, protecting the whole sometimes means removing one. Yes, it may hurt. But not acting hurts everyone more.

Leadership is not just about lifting people up. It is about knowing when someone is pulling the team down and having the courage to cut the rope.

Because while you may be saving them from short-term discomfort, you are sacrificing everyone else to long-term dysfunction.

What Happens When You Let Them Go

Something sacred happens.

The air clears. The team exhales. The good people stay. The culture resets. You, you feel strong again. You remember why you started this business. You feel proud of how you protected it.

Here is the beauty: once the toxicity is gone, the good starts to rise. Often, you will see a quiet employee step into new leadership. Someone who was shrinking now stands taller. Because the shadow is gone.

You did not just fire someone. You freed everyone else.

A Final Word on Second Chances

Second chances are beautiful, but not when they come at the cost of your business, your team, or your mental well-being.

Give them once, maybe twice. But after that, you are not being generous. You are being unfair, to everyone else.

Toxicity does not leave on its own. It must be named. Faced. And, when needed, released.

Not out of punishment, but protection. Not out of fear, but strength. Not out of anger, but grace.

That is how a leader saves their organization.

Chapter 10

Last Chance Leadership
What to Try Before
You Let Them Go

Before you make the final call, consider:

- A written **performance improvement plan** with a 30-day review.

- A peer mentor or "buddy system" for coaching.

- Offering **mental health resources** or time-off to reset.

- Mediation if conflict is interpersonal.

- A final **clarity conversation**, asking: *"Do you truly want to be here?"*

Sometimes, the answer is a quiet no, and they leave before you have to ask.

What If...? Quick Answers to Tough Moments:

- What if they cry? Let them. Be quiet. Then gently close the meeting.

- What if they accuse you of discrimination? Stay calm, document everything, and consult an attorney.

- What if your team disagrees? Remind them: your job is to lead the whole, not just appease parts.

- What if they are relative? Same rules apply. Blood does not excuse bad behavior. It just makes the goodbye harder, and more necessary.

The Leader's Documentation Checklist

Keep a simple folder for each employee that

includes:

- Signed offer letter.
- Job description.
- Signed handbook acknowledgment.
- Notes on verbal warnings or check-ins.
- Written warnings (with dates).
- Performance reviews.
- Any employee-initiated requests or concerns.

This protects you. It also makes difficult decisions more grounded in fact, not frustration.

Sample Exit Notes Template

Employee Name: _____

Date of Termination: _____

Reason (Brief):

_____

_____

Final Pay Includes: _____

Company Property Returned: _____

_____

Notes from Exit Meeting: _____

_____

_____

Leader's Signature: _____

Note: Document any and all correspondence. Keep it clear, factual, and respectful.

Chapter 11

When Loyalty
Becomes Liability

Loyalty is a beautiful word. It signals trust, longevity, and mutual respect. In a small business, loyalty often looks like that one employee who has been with you from the beginning, who knows your story, and who stood beside you through difficult seasons. But loyalty, when misunderstood or unchecked, can quietly shift from being an asset to becoming a liability.

Loyalty becomes a liability when it clouds your judgment. When you keep someone on the team not because they are right for the role, but because you feel you owe them. It becomes a liability when your commitment to history prevents you from doing what is right for the future.

This is not about betrayal or cold-hearted decisions. This is about leadership maturity. A good leader honors loyalty. A great leader knows when loyalty is quietly hurting the team.

The Loyalty Trap

In small businesses, lines blur quickly. Employees become like family. And that is not a bad thing. You share milestones. You celebrate birthdays. You support each other during personal crises. But when someone is no longer performing, no longer aligned, or no longer growing, the family bond becomes a trap. You find yourself tolerating behavior that you would not accept from a new hire.

You start making exceptions. You avoid hard conversations. You tell yourself, "They were there when no one else was."

But here is the truth: past loyalty does not excuse present dysfunction. You are not being disloyal by setting new standards. You are being responsible.

Because your loyalty to one person cannot override your responsibility to the rest of the team.

Signs That Loyalty Has Become Liability

1. Declining performance ignored. You notice the work quality slipping, but you avoid addressing it because of the employee's long history with you.

2. Resentment from others. Team members begin to question why one person is not held to the same expectations. Quiet frustration builds.

3. Stalled innovation. Loyal employees can sometimes resist change. Their comfort with the "way we have always done it" prevents growth.

4. Overdependence. You rely on them so heavily that you fear their departure. That fear keeps you from hiring or training others.

5. Avoidance of accountability. You offer gentle reminders instead of structured

feedback. You delay hard conversations because of shared history.

The Cost of Avoiding the Conversation:

When you let loyalty stand in the way of accountability, the entire culture pays the price. New employees see the double standard. High performers feel underappreciated. Mediocrity becomes the quiet norm.

You may think you are protecting someone, but you are really protecting a pattern that no longer serves the business. Worse, you may be doing a disservice to the loyal employee. Because sometimes, the most compassionate thing you can do is tell the truth.

Redefining Loyalty

Loyalty does not mean unconditional tolerance. It means mutual respect, honesty, and growth. A truly loyal employee wants to grow. They want feedback. They want the business to succeed, even if that means having hard conversations.

Redefine loyalty as something dynamic. Not as something that chains people to old versions of themselves, but as a partnership where both sides are committed to growth. That kind of loyalty strengthens a company. It pushes everyone forward.

How to Lead Through This Dilemma

1. Revisit the vision. Ask yourself: Does this person still align with where the business is going?

2. Have the honest talk. Set aside your emotional history and give clear, respectful feedback. Share what you appreciate. Then name what needs to change.

3. Create an improvement plan. Offer support, resources, and time. Make the expectations clear and measurable.

4. Be willing to release. If growth does not happen, honor the relationship by parting with dignity. You are not erasing history. You are choosing integrity.

5. Protect the culture. Remember that leadership is stewardship. You are responsible for the health of the whole, not just the comfort of one.

Compassion in Closure

If letting them go becomes the outcome, do it with compassion. Acknowledge the years. Thank them for their contribution. Make the exit honorable. Because loyalty, even when it is no longer aligned with the role, still deserves a graceful farewell.

The hardest decisions often reveal the strongest leaders. And choosing what is right over what is comfortable is one of the clearest signs of maturity. Your team will watch how you navigate loyalty. Let them see your courage. Let them see your compassion. Let them see your growth.

Because in the end, the business you are building deserves your loyalty too.

Chapter 12

The Myth of
the Irreplaceable Employee

Every business owner has heard it or felt it, "We cannot function without her." "He is the only one who knows how to do that." These phrases are whispered in moments of fear, usually when a long-standing employee threatens to leave, or when performance flags but consequences feel impossible. In these moments, the idea of the irreplaceable employee takes root. It sounds like admiration. But it often signals imbalance.

The truth is no one should be irreplaceable. Not because people are not valuable, but because systems and businesses should not be dependent on a single individual. That is not resilience, that is vulnerability.

When someone becomes the only person who holds a certain piece of knowledge, process, or control, it creates risk. If they leave, the business stumbles. If they underperform, accountability is blurred. If they resist change, progress halts. And still, leaders often hold on, afraid of the fallout, fearing disruption.

This fear-based loyalty reinforces a myth. But myths, by definition, are not meant to lead. Truth is.

Why the Myth Persists

Small businesses are built on trust and grit. The people who help in the early days often wear multiple hats, go above and beyond, and carry sacred knowledge of how things are done. Over time, this builds emotional capital. But sometimes, it builds walls around that person's role.

You stop cross-training others because they "will never do it like her." You overlook gaps because "he is doing so much already." You avoid restructuring because "it would be too disruptive." In trying to preserve what works, you unintentionally create a bottleneck.

And that bottleneck will hold your business hostage.

The Harm of Irreplaceability

1. Power Imbalance: When someone becomes irreplaceable, they gain unspoken power. Sometimes they use it responsibly. Sometimes they do not. But either way, it alters the workplace dynamic.

2. Stagnation: If only one person knows the system, you are one absence away from operational paralysis. Growth stalls. Innovation dries up.

3. Culture Shift: Other team members begin to feel undervalued. They notice who is protected. They notice who is allowed to break rules.

4. Leadership Avoidance: You stop leading. You start appeasing. Instead of building systems, you rely on people. Instead of empowering others, you feed dependency.

Turning the Myth Into a Lesson

You do not need to remove your most experienced person. You need to remove the illusion. The solution is not cutting people loose, it is building systems strong enough to stand without any single individual.

1. Cross-train rigorously. Every process should have at least one other person trained to execute it.

2. Document knowledge. Processes, contacts, steps, get them out of people's heads and into shared systems.

3. Rotate roles occasionally. Give others a chance to learn and lead. Stretch potential beyond comfort zones.

4. Set expectations early. Let your team know that growth comes with shared responsibility, not secret expertise.

5. Thank and transition. If someone resists this shift, meet them with gratitude and clarity. Honor their contribution. Invite them to evolve with you, or bless them as they move on.

Compassionate Leadership Is Collective Leadership

Compassion does not mean overdependence. It means care with boundaries. It means building teams that support each other, not just orbit around one star. It means knowing that your most valuable players are still part of a whole, and honoring that whole through preparation, process, and protection.

The myth of the irreplaceable employee fades when you choose growth over fear. When you believe in people, but also build for the future. When you honor contributions without becoming beholden to them.

The best teams are not built around one hero. They are built with shared strength. Your job is not to crown the irreplaceable. Your job is to raise the capable.

Lead with confidence. Build with structure. And never let the myth guide your mission.

Chapter 13

Is It Time To Let Them Go

There comes a moment, quiet, heavy, unmistakable, when you know.

You have given warnings. You have listened. You have offered support, direction, even second chances. You have waited longer than you should have. Now, something in you is still. Not angry. Not flustered. Just clear.

It is time to let them go.

This moment is not a failure. It is a sign of growth, your growth as a leader. It means you have moved past trying to fix what refuses to change, and you are ready to protect what remains.

Because leadership is not just about holding on. Sometimes it is about knowing when to release.

How You Know It Is Time

These are the signs that confirm what your gut already knows:

- The same behavior continues, even after conversations and consequences.

- Morale among other team members is dropping.

- Clients or customers are beginning to notice.

- You feel anxious, irritated, or drained every time that person walks in.

- You spend more time managing them than running your business.

- You have become someone you do not like, walking on eggshells, overcompensating, making excuses.

You may feel guilty. That is normal. But guilt does not mean you are wrong. It means you have a conscience. Use that conscience to do this right, but do not let it keep you in a place of inaction.

Letting Them Go Is Not Cruel

Keeping someone in a role where they cannot thrive, that is cruel.

Letting someone stay when their presence poisons the energy of the team, that is cruel.

Letting someone go, when done with honesty and grace, is often a gift. It tells the truth. It makes space for someone better aligned. It restores peace for the people who are still all in.

Sometimes, it gives the departing person the push they have long needed to change course.

Prepare Before You Act

Do not rush it. Prepare thoroughly:

- Review documentation and previous conversations.

- Have a final paycheck ready (including unused vacation or legally required payments).

- Understand your state's laws on termination, final pay, and benefits.

- Prepare a termination letter, simple, clear, factual.

- Choose the right time and place, quiet, private, uninterrupted.

Decide this in advance:

Will they leave immediately?

Will they finish the day? The week?

Think through what is best for your business and your people.

Stay Calm, Direct, and Brief

Begin with clarity:

- "We've had several conversations about performance and expectations. Unfortunately, there hasn't been enough improvement, and we've decided to move on."

- "Today will be your last day with us. This decision is final."

- "Here's your final paycheck and a letter confirming your separation."

Avoid long explanations or arguments. Be kind, but do not get pulled into negotiation. The decision is made.

They may be shocked. They may get emotional. They may try to argue. Let them speak, if it helps them release the moment, but do not change your message. Do not debate. Hold your ground with grace.

Respect Their Dignity

Even if they have been difficult, do this with dignity. No shaming. No gossip later. No angry tone. You are not seeking revenge. You are closing a chapter, with peace.

- Allow them space to collect their things with privacy.

- If appropriate, thank them for their contributions.

- Let the rest of the team know briefly and professionally that the person is no longer with the company.

Your other employees will remember how you handled it. Do it in a way you can be proud of.

You May Feel Relief, and That Is Okay

After it is done, you might feel a deep breath escape your body. A weight gone. That is not cruelty, it is release. You have held it together for longer than people knew. You carried more stress than you admitted. Now, you have done the right thing.

Let the relief come.

Leadership requires courage. Letting someone go is not just about protecting your business, it is about freeing everyone from a cycle that no longer works. So, if this moment has arrived for you, know this: You are not heartless. You are, finally, fully leading.

Chapter 14

The Exit Conversation

There is no easy way to look someone in the eye and say, "It is time for you to go."

Even when the decision is justified, even when it is long overdue, it still lands heavy. Why? Because behind every employee is a human story. A livelihood. A routine. Behind every employer, there is a heart that wishes it did not come to this.

When handled with clarity, dignity, and calm, the exit conversation can become more than a goodbye. It can be a final act of leadership. A moment of truth that brings closure, not chaos.

Here is how to do it well.

The Tone: Calm, Clear, Final

This is not the moment for surprise lectures or drawn-out speeches. This is not where you retell the full history of what went wrong.

The decision has been made. The tone should match that certainty. Steady. Respectful. Clean.

Speak slowly, breathe fully, and hold the space with composure.

Begin with a direct opening:

- "Thank you for taking a moment to meet. I want to let you know that we've decided to end your employment here, effective today."

- "We've spoken about expectations and challenges in recent weeks, and unfortunately, the improvements haven't been enough. We're moving forward without your role."

That is it.

No dramatic pause.

No invitation to debate. You are informing, not consulting.

Anticipate Reactions, But Do not Absorb Them

Expect one of the following:

- Silence. It may come with shock, even if they saw it coming.

- Sadness. Some may tear up or feel shame. Offer a tissue, a pause, but not pity. Lead with care and compassion.

- Anger. Stay calm. Do not defend, argue, or explain beyond your initial statement.

- Blame. You may hear, "You never gave me a real chance" or "This is unfair." Acknowledge briefly but stand firm.

Remember, you do not have to fix their feelings. You only have to deliver the decision with grace.

What to Say Next

After your opening, move swiftly into the logistics:

- "Today is your last day. Here is your final paycheck, including unused vacation time."

- "Your benefits will continue through [date], and you will receive COBRA information separately."

- "Here is a written summary of your separation."

- "Please take a few minutes to collect your things. Let me know if you prefer someone to assist or if you'd like privacy."

Provide a short-written notice that includes:

- The effective date.

- Their final pay and how it was calculated.

- Any return-of-property expectations.

- Contact information for final HR questions (or yours, if you are the point of contact).

Leave the Door Open, Only If Authentic

Sometimes, especially when the person was not a good fit but was not malicious, it is appropriate to end on a kind note:

- "I know this may be difficult, but I hope you find the right place where you can thrive."

- "We wish you the best in your next chapter."

But only say these things if you mean them. Forced niceties do more harm than good.

What to Say to the Team

After the employee exits, address the remaining team:

- Keep it brief.

- Stay professional.

- Never speak poorly about the person who left.

Try this:

- "I want to let you know that [Name] is no longer with us as of today. We thank them for their contributions and wish them well. Please come to me with any questions or concerns. Let us all keep things respectful and professional as we move forward."

This models maturity and prevents gossip from taking over.

Do not Linger

After the conversation, release it. You did your job. You led with courage. You ended what needed to end.

You are not cruel. You are not careless. You are a leader, one who chose to act with integrity rather than prolong the inevitable.

You did it with grace.

Chapter 15

Let Them Go
Keep Your Humanity

At the end of it all, HR is not just about policies, documentation, or legal safeguards. It is about people, how we understand them, how we support them, and how we let them go when the time comes.

Letting someone go will never be easy. It should not be. But it can be done with dignity. It can be done with courage. And most importantly, it can be done without losing your soul in the process.

To lead is to hold tension, the tension between protecting the business and protecting the humanity within it. You will be challenged. You will face moments where your heart aches, where your judgment is tested, where your compassion is mistaken for weakness. Hold your ground.

The small business owner who leads with values, who stays true to their vision, who hires with intention and lets go with grace, that is the leader who builds not just a company, but a culture.

If you have read this far, you are already that kind of leader, or on your way there. This book was never about telling you what to do. It was about reminding you who you are.

You are the kind of person who cares enough to pause, to listen, to think things through. You are the kind of leader who believes that doing the right thing is worth it, even when no one is watching.

So when the moment comes, when you face a difficult choice, a hard conversation, a letting go, remember this:

You do not have to be perfect. You just have to be present. You do not need all the answers. You just need to show up with integrity.

Let them go. But keep your humanity.

Chapter 16

After the Goodbye

The door has closed. The employee has left. What remains is silence, brief, but thick.

You did what had to be done. But now you are left with the part no one talks about. The clean-up. The questions. The energy shift in the room. You may feel relief. You may feel guilt. You may even feel a strange grief, the kind that comes from the weight of finality.

This chapter is about what comes next. Because letting someone go is only the midpoint of the process. What you do afterward determines whether your team heals or hardens, whether your business regains balance or spirals in uncertainty.

This is where leadership deepens.

Take a Breath. You Need It.

Before you talk to the team, before you return to normal, take a moment.

Sit. Breathe. Let your body catch up with your courage. The exit conversation took something from you. Even if it was necessary. Even if it was overdue. Give yourself a quiet minute.

You do not have to be a machine. You are human. You acted with care. Let yourself feel what that took.

Tend to the Team Quickly, Gently

The remaining employees are watching. Not to judge, but to understand. They are wondering what this means for them, for the business, for the culture.

Call a short team meeting, ideally within the hour.

Say something like:

- "As you know, [Name] is no longer with the company. We're moving forward with some adjustments. I want you to know this decision was not taken lightly. It was about alignment and performance, not personal feelings."

- "We will shift some tasks around and make sure no one feels overwhelmed. If you have questions or ideas, my door is open."

This gives people permission to feel unsettled without feeding drama. You are showing strength and openness at once.

Protect Morale Without Sugarcoating

Avoid vague reassurances like "Everything's fine." People know when something is not. Instead, focus on the path forward:

- "We're going to take this moment to strengthen how we communicate and support one another."

- "This is a good time to revisit our values and how we hold each other accountable."

You are not covering up the wound. You are helping it close with care.

Redistribute Work Intentionally

Do not just dump the departing employee's tasks onto someone else. Ask:

- What can be paused for now?

- What needs immediate coverage?

- Who has capacity, and who does not?

Consider temporary solutions before committing to a new hire. Let things settle. Often, teams naturally realign in a healthier way when one toxic or misaligned presence is gone.

Let Gossip Die Before It Starts

Nip gossip immediately. If you hear whispers, confront them privately but firmly:

- "We're not going to speculate about someone's exit. That is not how we do things here."

- "If you have a concern, come talk to me directly."

This protects your culture. It teaches that respect does not end when employment does.

Support Quiet Grievers

Sometimes, even if someone was not a great employee, they were still liked. A friend. A familiar face. And now they are gone.

Watch for team members who may be sad, shaken, or anxious. Check in with them. Let them talk. Validate the feeling without second-guessing the decision.

- "I know this change may feel sudden. It is okay to feel a mix of things. Let me know how you are doing."

When people feel seen, they stay steady.

Reflect on the Process, Privately

Once things have quieted down, reflect:

- Did I act too late?

- Did I communicate clearly enough along the way?

- What warning signs did I miss or ignore?

- What can I do differently with the next hire?

This is not about blame. It is about refinement. Every decision teaches you something. Let it.

Lead Like the Future Just Began

Do not dwell. Do not apologize to yourself for doing what was right.

Today marks a fresh start, not just for the business, but for you as a leader.

You have done what many will not. You have held space for conflict without collapsing. You have led through discomfort without turning cold.

That is not just HR. That is heart. Congratulations. It is rare.

Chapter 17

Compassion Under Pressure

For every leader who ever lost sleep over a hard decision, may this book help you lead with a clearer mind, a stronger voice, and an unshakable heart.

Pressure does not ask permission to enter the room; it walks in unannounced. In the world of small business, where the margins are tight and the team is close, pressure is not occasional. It is constant. And how a leader responds to it defines not just the mood of the moment but the culture of the company.

Some leaders react. Others respond. But the ones who endure and uplift do something different: they hold compassion under pressure.

Compassion is not weakness. It is not smiling through difficulty or pretending everything is fine.

Compassion is strength wrapped in calm. It is the ability to stay clear-minded when decisions need to be made fast. It is the power to remain kind when every part of you is being pulled in opposing directions. Compassion under pressure is what separates bosses from leaders. And in a small business, your compassion becomes your team's permission to breathe.

Compassion Is the Tone of Leadership

A team can read your face faster than they read the room. When your voice tightens, when your energy shifts, when frustration escapes through your sighs, they feel it. Even if you do not say a word, they absorb your state. And then they mirror it.

You may not realize it, but you are the emotional thermostat of your business. When you carry compassion in a stressful moment, it regulates the temperature for everyone else. People stop spiraling. They ground themselves. They get back to thinking instead of reacting.

Compassion does not mean being passive. It means choosing to lead from clarity, not chaos.

A client is yelling. A shipment did not arrive. Payroll hit a snag. You still hold your posture. You ask the right questions. You reassure your team, not with hollow words, but with calm presence. That is compassion in motion.

There will be moments when you are overwhelmed. You will be tired. You will be triggered. You will want to lash out, raise your voice, or storm into a room with demands. But leadership begins the moment you pause.

In that pause, you remind yourself: I am not here to explode. I am here to lead and inspire.

Your role is not to avoid pressure. It is to meet it

differently. With preparation. With awareness. With empathy. You do not need all the answers. But you do need to show up in a way that helps others find theirs.

That does not mean you never cry, vent, or falter. You are human. But it means you return to center faster. You model recovery. You model self-control. You lead.

A culture of fear can be built in a single week of poorly handled stress. All it takes is a few panic-driven decisions, a loud blowup, or a passive-aggressive meltdown, and suddenly, your team does not feel safe.

They tiptoe. They second-guess. They withhold ideas because they do not want to be snapped at. They leave early to avoid your mood. And if that continues, your business becomes a place they survive, not thrive.

Compassion, on the other hand, builds a culture of trust. It teaches your team that yes, things will go wrong, but no, they will not be humiliated or blamed for it. That does not mean you avoid accountability. It means you handle mistakes without emotional harm. That is leadership maturity.

Practical Ways to Practice Compassion

1. Respond in five breaths, not five words. When you are hit with a problem, pause. Breathe. Speak after you have calmed your first reaction.

2. Separate emotion from instruction. You can be upset internally without letting that emotion spill into every interaction. Say, "I am frustrated by the situation, not with you personally."

3. Hold private corrections, not public shaming. If someone messes up, take it

behind closed doors. Dignity matters more in small spaces.

4. Do not make decisions at your peak emotion. Give yourself a few hours or a day before sending that email or enforcing that new rule.

5. Check in with yourself before checking out on others. Say, "Am I tired? Triggered?

6. Overwhelmed? Or am I actually responding to what is in front of me?"

Compassion under pressure does something remarkable: it creates followers who eventually become leaders themselves. Why? Because they learn not just how to handle problems, but how to carry people through them.

They remember how you did not raise your voice. How you asked instead of accused. How you prioritized resolution over ego. And when it is their turn to lead, they will mirror the same.

Compassion multiplies. That is its secret power.

One day, when your business is bigger or your role changes, people will not remember the specifics of what went wrong on that chaotic Thursday afternoon. But they will remember you.

They will remember how you treated them when things were tight. When mistakes were made. When deadlines were missed. When nerves were high. They will remember if you lifted the atmosphere or made it heavier.

Compassion is not always loud. It does not always get applause. But it leaves a lasting memorable imprint.

Chapter 18

Suspend Your Judgment HR The Heart of the Organization

HR is often described as a rulebook, a compliance tool, or a mechanism to protect the business. But the most effective HR practices come not from policies, but from presence, from the ability of a leader to stay open, even in discomfort. At the center of that presence is the ability to suspend judgment.

To suspend judgment does not mean you never decide. It means you pause, observe, and listen before acting. It means you acknowledge your emotional reactions without letting them drive your decisions. It is not passive. It is active restraint, the hallmark of wisdom.

In human-centered HR, this becomes a daily practice. Whether you are hiring, managing, reviewing, or letting someone go, the greatest harm is often done by rushing to conclusions. The greatest healing often begins when we wait, witness, and understand.

Why We Rush to Judge

Humans are wired for efficiency. We love shortcuts, patterns, and quick conclusions. In HR, this can become dangerous:

- We assume someone is lazy based on one missed deadline.

- We believe someone is dishonest based on a single misunderstanding.

- We label an employee as "difficult" because they challenged a policy.

But employees are human beings, not fixed data points. Their behavior is often shaped by things we do not see, grief, anxiety, fear, trauma, or unspoken workplace dynamics.

When you suspend judgment, you create the space to learn what else might be true.

From Reactivity to Inquiry

Suspending judgment allows you to move from reaction to curiosity:

- Instead of "Why did you do that?" try "Can you walk me through what happened?"

- Instead of "That's unacceptable," ask "Is there something that made this difficult for you?"

- Instead of jumping into consequences, begin with connection.

This shift transforms not just the outcomes, but the relationship.

Compassion Without Compromise

Pausing judgment does not mean tolerating harm. If someone is abusive, unsafe, or consistently violating expectations, action must be taken. But even that action can come from clarity, not reactivity.

When HR suspends judgment:

- Investigations are more balanced.

- Feedback is more thoughtful.

- Firings are more humane.

- Trust becomes a cultural norm.

The employees who stay feel safer. The ones who go feel respected. And the business stands on the foundation of integrity, not impulse.

The Power of the Pause

To lead HR well, especially in a small business, you need more than rules. You need discernment. And discernment is born in the pause:

- The pause before responding to an emotional outburst.

- The pause before sending a corrective email.

- The pause before letting someone go.

That pause is not weakness. It is mastery. It is how we protect people from being judged by our worst moments, or our worst moods.

Final Thought

When you suspend judgment, you create room for truth to emerge. You become a leader, people can trust. You handle HR not just with your head, but with your heart.

In doing so, you build a workplace where fairness is not just a promise, it is a lived practice.

Chapter 19

Difficult Conversations Done Right

The hardest conversations are often the ones that matter most. In the workplace, few things test a leader's growth and compassion more than addressing behavior, performance, or exit discussions with honesty and empathy. For small business owners, these conversations often feel personal, uncomfortable, and even risky. But they are also the gateway to clarity, trust, and long-term stability.

Difficult conversations are not a punishment; they are a responsibility. They are the moment when leadership becomes visible. This chapter offers practical tools and emotional grounding to help business owners approach hard conversations with courage, structure, and care.

Why We Avoid Them

Most people avoid difficult conversations because they fear three things: hurting feelings, making things worse, or not knowing what to say. But avoidance rarely brings peace. It creates silence, resentment, and confusion. In business, that translates into poor performance, cultural drift, and sometimes, bigger problems down the line.

When leaders delay conversations, they sacrifice clarity. When they speak up with courage and compassion, they offer the gift of truth, even if it is hard to hear.

Prepare Before You Speak

A powerful conversation starts before a single word is said. Preparation is not about scripting every line, it is about anchoring your intent and clarifying your facts.

Ask yourself:

- What behavior or pattern needs to change?

- Do I have clear examples?

- What impact is it having on the team or business?

- What outcome am I hoping for?

- Am I open to hearing their side?

Then, choose a private space. Pick a time when neither of you are rushed. And begin from a place of purpose, not blame.

A Simple Framework

Here is a conversation framework you can adapt:

1. State the concern.

"I want to talk with you about something important that is affecting the team."

2. Share the impact.

   "When deadlines are missed, it delays the entire project and causes stress for others."

3. Invite their perspective.

   "How do you see it? Is something going on that I should know about?"

4. Clarify expectations.

   "We need to make sure this does not continue. What support would help you meet the deadlines consistently?"

5. End with dignity.

   "I want you to succeed here. Let us find a way forward together."

Tone Over Script

Words matter. But tone matters more. Your voice, posture, and presence communicate just as much as your phrases. Speak with calm, not force. Make eye contact. Pause when needed. Listen without interrupting.

People may forget what you said, but they will remember how you made them feel.

When Things Get Emotional

Tears, frustration, silence, these are normal. Do not rush to fill the space. Let the person process. Then gently guide the conversation back to purpose and solutions.

If the discussion becomes too heated or off track, it is okay to pause and reschedule. "Let us take a break and continue this tomorrow when we have both had time to reflect."

Document Briefly After

After the conversation, write a short summary. This is not just for legal protection, it is for clarity. Include what was discussed, any commitments made, and a follow-up plan. Keep it in the employee file.

Why It Matters

Difficult conversations, done right, change everything. They create turning points. They reveal values. They reinforce culture.

When you choose to engage rather than avoid, you model what courage looks like. You teach your team that honesty and kindness can coexist.

Letting someone go may be the final act. But often, it is these conversations that determine whether that moment arrives at all.

Speak early. Speak clearly. Speak kindly. That is how leaders move through discomfort, without losing compassion.

Chapter 20

Documentation Is Protection

In the world of small business, most decisions are made on the fly. Owners juggle operations, customer relations, finances, and people, all in one day. There is little time for formalities, and even less patience for paperwork. But when it comes to human resources, one truth stands above all: what you do not document can come back to hurt you.

Documentation is not bureaucracy. It is protection, for the employee, for the owner, and for the business itself. It creates clarity. It captures history. It provides evidence of fairness. And in the event of conflict, complaint, or legal scrutiny, it becomes your shield.

Why Documentation Matters

1. Memory is flawed. We forget dates. We misremember conversations. We reconstruct stories. Documentation ensures that facts stay facts.

2. Fairness requires records. If two employees are treated differently, documentation helps explain why. Without it, fairness looks like favoritism.

3. Legal defense depends on it. If an employee challenges a termination or files a claim, written documentation can show due process and good faith.

4. Growth stems from reflection.

   Documented feedback helps employees track their development. It also helps leaders see patterns and improve management.

What to Document

You do not need to document everything. But you do need to document the right things. Here is what should be part of every HR file:

- Job descriptions and signed offer letters

- Written expectations and policy acknowledgments

- Performance reviews and check-ins

- Any disciplinary notices or corrective actions

- Attendance issues or behavioral concerns

- Emails or written memos related to performance

Keep it factual. Avoid opinions. Stick to observable behavior and outcomes.

How to Document Effectively

1. Be timely. Document issues or conversations soon after they occur. Delay weakens accuracy.

2. Be specific. Use dates, examples, and direct quotes when possible. Vague notes help no one.

3. Be respectful. Even when noting concerns, write with professionalism. This document may be read by others.

4. Have the employee sign. This does not mean they agree, it means they have been informed. Their signature protects you both.

5. Store securely. Keep HR documents private and organized. Only authorized individuals should have access.

When Documentation Is Missing

When there is no paper trail, everything becomes hearsay. You might know in your heart that you acted fairly, gave warnings, or offered support. But in business, feelings do not hold up, records do.

And documentation is not just for bad news. Keep records of praise, promotions, and achievements.

Show the full picture. Let your employees know they are seen, not only when there is a problem.

Small Business, Big Responsibility

In large companies, entire HR departments handle documentation. But in a small business, it is often up to the owner. That does not mean it has to be perfect. It just has to be consistent.

Make documentation part of your leadership rhythm. After every coaching talk, take five minutes to jot a summary. After every review, capture the goals. Build a habit of recording what matters. It is an act of accountability. It is an act of compassion.

Documentation says, "This matters enough to remember." And in the life of a business, that memory could one day make all the difference.

Write it down. Keep it clear. Let it protect you, now and later.

Chapter 21

Legal Considerations Without Fear

Small business owners often fear the legal side of human resources. Words like "wrongful termination," "harassment claim," or "compliance" can feel intimidating. But fear, when left unaddressed, becomes avoidance, and avoidance leads to costly mistakes. You do not need to be a lawyer to protect your business. You simply need awareness, intention, and a willingness to ask for help when needed. Please inquire about my book, *Protect Your Business, Stay Informed, Stay Ahead*, for additional Tax and Business insights.

The goal is not to operate from fear, but from confidence. Confidence comes from clarity. And clarity begins with understanding the most essential legal principles every small business owner should know.

Start With the Basics

1. At-will employment still has limits. While most states follow at-will employment, meaning an employer can terminate an employee for any reason or no reason at all, there are still important exceptions. You cannot fire someone for a discriminatory reason or in retaliation for asserting a legal right.

2. Document before you decide. As covered in the previous chapter, documentation is your best defense. If you ever need to justify a decision, whether in a mediation, audit, or court, your written record is the story that matters.

3. Final pay matters. Each state has laws about

4. when and how to deliver a final paycheck. Late or incomplete final pay can lead to penalties, even if the termination itself was lawful.

5. Classify correctly. Misclassifying an employee as an independent contractor, or incorrectly labeling someone as exempt from overtime, can lead to fines and back pay. Know the definitions. Ask an HR consultant or accountant if you are unsure.

6. Harassment claims are everyone's business. You cannot ignore employee complaints, even if they seem minor. A pattern of neglecting complaints, even informal ones, can turn into a hostile work environment claim.

Common Legal Pitfalls to Avoid

- Firing someone on the spot without cause or conversation.

- Letting someone go after they report a problem without clear documentation of unrelated performance issues.

- Not providing written policies or an employee handbook.

- Making verbal promises that contradict written documents.

- Failing to offer final pay, PTO payout (if required), or benefits information.

Ask Before You Act

The smartest leaders know when to slow down and consult. You do not need to know everything, but you do need to know when to pick up the phone.

Before making a termination decision:

- Review the employee's file. Is there documentation?

- Look at timing. Is there any recent protected activity?

- Call your HR advisor, employment attorney, or business association hotline.

Even a 15-minute consult could save you thousands and protect your business.

Compliance Is Not About Fear

Compliance is not red tape. It is respect, for the employee, the business, and the process. Most lawsuits are not born out of the action itself but out of how the person felt treated. When people feel heard, respected, and fairly handled, the risk of legal escalation drops dramatically.

Clarity is kindness. Consistency is power. Courage is doing the right thing even when it takes a few extra steps.

When You Are in the Right, Do Not Be Afraid

Letting someone go is hard. But when you have followed the process, communicated clearly, documented consistently, and treated the person with compassion, you can walk forward without fear.

You will not win every battle in life, but if you lead with integrity and knowledge, you will win the war for your business's longevity and reputation.

Take the time. Get the guidance. Then let them go, like a leader, not from fear, but from wisdom.

Chapter 22

The Importance of HR in an HR Environment

HR is not a checkbox, it is a cornerstone. In any business, and especially in a small business, human resources is the foundation of how people are hired, managed, supported, and eventually let go. While many leaders think of HR as paperwork or compliance, the truth is more profound: HR shapes culture, protects people, and ensures that the business runs not just legally, but ethically.

In an HR environment, where responsibilities are often blurred between operations, leadership, and people management, the importance of a structured, value-based HR approach cannot be overstated. This chapter explores why HR matters, how it shows up day-to-day, and what every small business leader must know to honor the human side of the work.

More Than Hiring and Firing

Human Resources is often reduced to recruitment and termination, but its true role is far deeper. HR is involved in every stage of the employee lifecycle:

- Attracting the right talent.
- Crafting clear roles and expectations.
- Supporting onboarding and development.
- Handling conflict resolution.
- Encouraging growth and learning.
- Navigating leaves, benefits, and transitions.
- Protecting the business from legal exposure.

When done with care, HR creates a healthy workplace. When ignored or rushed, it breeds confusion, mistrust, and instability.

The HR Environment in Small Business

In large organizations, HR teams and specialists take the lead. In small businesses, the owner or manager often handles these duties directly. This makes the environment more intimate, but also more vulnerable to oversight or bias.

- Are expectations clearly documented?

- Do employees know their rights and responsibilities?

- Are there systems in place to address complaints or feedback?

- Are reviews fair, regular, and documented?

Without intentional HR practices, even the kindest leaders can make mistakes that lead to legal, financial, or emotional costs.

An HR Mindset

To thrive in an HR environment, leaders must develop an HR mindset. This means asking, in every decision: "What is best for the employee, and best for the business?

It means:

- Balancing empathy with accountability.

- Using data and documentation, not just feelings.

- Addressing issues early rather than avoiding them.

- Creating equity and consistency across the team.

An HR mindset is not about becoming rigid. It is about becoming reliable.

The Risk of Neglect

When HR is treated as an afterthought, businesses suffer. Poor hiring decisions, toxic work environments, mishandled exits, these create real harm. They lead to turnover, legal action, and reputation damage. More importantly, they violate the trust that employees place in their leaders.

You do not need to be perfect. But you do need to care. And caring means learning, preparing, and investing in the human processes of your business.

The Benefit of Intentionality

Intentional HR practices lead to:

- Higher employee morale.

- Clearer roles and expectations.

- Fewer misunderstandings or conflicts.

- Smoother transitions in times of change.

- A reputation as a place where people want to work.

You do not need a full HR department to lead with excellence. You need courage, organization, and heart.

Closing Thought

Human Resources is not about bureaucracy. It is about people. When you honor the human side of your business, everything works better. People stay longer, perform better, and speak more positively about their work.

In an HR environment, especially a small business one, the question is not whether HR is present, it is whether it is healthy. Let your HR practices reflect the values you hold. Let them become part of how you lead.

That is what it means to build a business with care, with clarity, and with compassion.

Recommended Readings

Goleman, D. (1995). *Emotional intelligence: Why it can matter more than IQ.* New York, NY: Bantam Books.

Khoureis, A. (2022-2025). *The Compassionate Leadership Model and Pyramid.* ANG Power Publishing House.

Khoureis, A. (2025). *The Seven Secrets of Exceptional Mentorship.* ANG Power Publishing House.

Khoureis, A. (2025). *Microaggressions for Leaders & Beyond: Understanding Microaggressions Face-To-Face.* Inclusive Wisdom Press.

Khoureis, A. (2025). *Protecting Your Business: Stay Informed, Stay Ahead.* Insightful Tax and Business Ideas for Small Business Owners. ANG Power Publishing House

Society for Human Resource Management. (2022). *SHRM essentials of human resources*. Alexandria, VA: SHRM.

Ulrich, D. (1997). *Human resource champions: The next agenda for adding value and delivering results*. Boston, MA: Harvard Business School Press.

Ulrich, D., Brockbank, W., Johnson, D., Sandholtz, K., & Younger, J. (2008).

HR competencies: Mastery at the intersection of people and business. Alexandria, VA: Society for Human Resource Management.

Ulrich, D., & Dulebohn, J. H. (2015). Are we there yet? What is next for HR? *Human Resource Management*, 54(2), 159–171. https://doi.org/10.1002/hrm.21710

About Dr. Abraham Khoureis, Ph.D.

Dr. Abraham Khoureis, Ph.D., is a multi-talented thought leader and partner, author, an award-winning mentor, and advocate for compassionate leadership. He is an adjunct professor who specializes in teaching graduate-level courses in business and management, blending academic theory with real-world business practices. Dr. Khoureis is also a small business owner and holds numerous state certifications and professional designations and licenses, showcasing his multidisciplinary expertise.

He is the creator of the Compassionate Leadership Model and Pyramid, which emphasizes leadership built on self-awareness, mindfulness, and commitment to serving others without expectation of return. This seven-level model pyramid, with "Community" as its 5th level, reflects his vision of leadership that positively impacts the broader community and society.

Moreover, Dr. Khoureis developed the Disability Learning Attainment Model, a framework designed to empower individuals with disabilities through inclusive education, skill-building, and leadership development. His work champions and empowers inclusivity, accessibility, and ethical practices in both education and leadership. He has been published on *Forbes.com*, *Newsweek.com*, and the distinguished *Leader to Leader Journal*. He was recognized as LinkedIn's Top Leadership and Management Voice, and Thinkers 360's Top 50 Voices.

Dr. Abe's contributions extend to his writings, professional development initiatives, and thought leadership, making him a respected emerging leader in the fields of compassionate leadership, organizational behavior, and human development.

Easily accessible at: DrAbeKhoureis.com
Social Media: @DrAbeKhoureis
DrAbeBooks.com

Other Books by Dr. Abraham Khoureis, Ph.D.

The Balance In Between: Finding the Balance Between Emotional Intelligence and Emotional Stupidity
ISBN: 979-8-9895211-2-8

Decoding Microaggressions for Leaders and Beyond: Understanding Microaggressions Face-to-Face
ISBN: 979-8-9895211-4-2

Hollywood Dream: How To Make It In Tinseltown
ISBN: 979-8-9895211-7-3

Protect Your Business: Stay Informed, Stay Ahead
ISBN: 978-1-966837-09-1

Reasonable Accommodation: Empowering Inclusion
ISBN: 979-8-9895211-3-5

Revealing the Seven Secrets to Exceptional Mentorship
ISBN: 978-1-966837-00-8

SELF: Introducing The Self Rotating Model
ISBN: 979-8-9895211-5-9

The Compassionate Leadership Model and Pyramid
ISBN: 979-8-9895211-0-4

This page intentionally left blank for your final reading reflection

_____

_____

_____

_____

_____

_____

_____

_____

_____

_____

LET THEM GO LIKE A LEADER

DR. ABRAHAM KHOUREIS, PH.D.

www.ingramcontent.com/pod-product-compliance
Lightning Source LLC
Chambersburg PA
CBHW060606200326
41521CB00007B/674